USHER

RIGHT ON!

Gareth Stevens
Publishing

By Therese Shea

Please visit our Web site, www.garethstevens.com. For a free color catalog of all our high-quality books, call toll free 1-800-542-2595 or fax 1-877-542-2596.

Library of Congress Cataloging-in-Publication Data

Shea, Therese.
 Usher / Therese Shea.
    p. cm. — (Hip-hop headliners)
 Includes index.
 ISBN 978-1-4339-4812-1 (library binding)
 ISBN 978-1-4339-4813-8 (pbk.)
 ISBN 978-1-4339-4814-5 (6-pack)
 1. Usher—Juvenile literature. 2. Rhythm and blues musicians—United States—
Biography—Juvenile literature. 3. Singers—United States—Biography—Juvenile literature.
I. Title.
 ML3930.U84S54 2011
 782.421643092—dc22
 [B]
                              2010030118

First Edition

Published in 2011 by
Gareth Stevens Publishing
111 East 14th Street, Suite 349
New York, NY 10003

Copyright © 2011 Gareth Stevens Publishing

Designer: Haley W. Harasymiw
Editor: Therese Shea

Photo credits: Cover, pp. 2–32 (background) Shutterstock.com; cover (Usher), p. 1 Michael Loccisano/Getty Images; p. 5 Frederick M. Brown/Getty Images; p. 7 Mario Tama/Getty Images; pp. 9, 13, 21 Frank Micelotta/Getty Images; p. 11 Dave Hogan/Getty Images; p. 15 Frank Micelotta/Image Direct; p. 17 Alex Wong/Getty Images; p. 19 Evan Agostini/Getty Images; pp. 23, 27, 29 Scott Gries/Getty Images; p. 25 Bryan Bedder/Getty Images.

Printed in the United States of America

CPSIA compliance information: Batch #CW11GS: For further information contact Gareth Stevens, New York, New York at 1-800-542-2595.

Contents

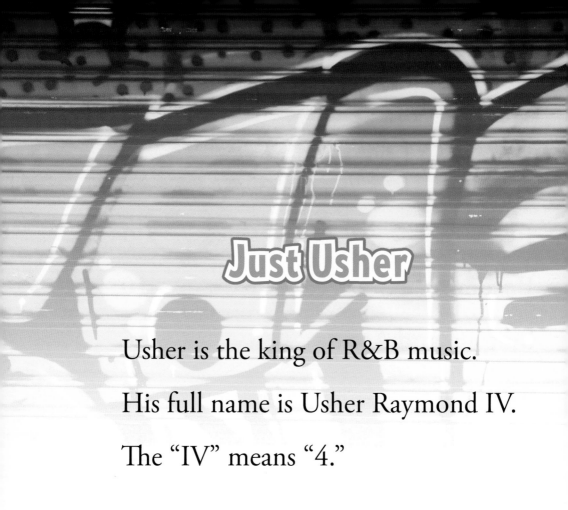

Just Usher

Usher is the king of R&B music.

His full name is Usher Raymond IV.

The "IV" means "4."

On October 14, 1978, Usher was born in Dallas, Texas. His family moved to Tennessee. Then they moved to Georgia.

When he was 9 years old, Usher began to sing in his church. He decided to be a singer when he grew up.

Becoming a Star

In 1991, Usher sang on the TV show *Star Search*. A man from a music business saw him. He asked Usher to make an album.

Usher called his first album *Usher*.

He worked on it with hip-hop star

Sean Combs. Usher became famous.

He was just 15 years old!

Sean Combs

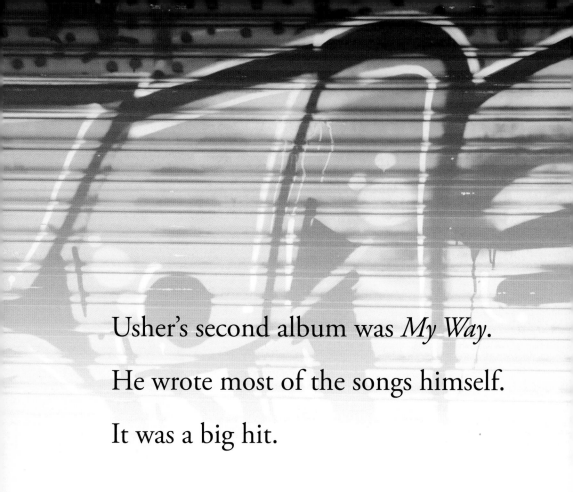

Usher's second album was *My Way*.

He wrote most of the songs himself.

It was a big hit.

Singing and Acting

Usher acted in TV shows. He was in *Moesha* with music star Brandy. He was in movies, such as *She's All That*.

Usher loved acting. However, he still made music. His third album was *8701*. He won two Grammys for it.

19

In 2004, Usher's *Confessions* sold over 1 million albums in a week. He sang the song "Yeah!" with hip-hop stars Lil Jon and Ludacris.

Lil Jon

Ludacris

In 2006, Usher starred in the musical *Chicago* in New York City. He sang and acted each night in front of a lot of people. He loved it!

23

Usher has his own music business called US Label. One of his biggest acts is singer Justin Bieber.

Justin Bieber

Usher keeps making music. In 2008, his album *Here I Stand* was number one on the charts.

Usher's 2010 album reached number one, too. He worked with will.i.am to make the song "OMG." It was a hit all over the world.

will.i.am

29

Timeline

1978   Usher Raymond IV is born on October 14 in Dallas, Texas.

1991   Usher wins on *Star Search*.

1994   Usher's first album comes out.

1997   Usher stars in *Moesha*.

2001   Usher's Grammy-winning album *8701* comes out.

2004   *Confessions* becomes Usher's biggest album.

2010   Usher's album *Raymond v. Raymond* becomes number one.

For More Information

Books:

Adams, Colleen. *Usher*. New York, NY: PowerKids Press, 2007.

Lord, Raymond. *Usher*. Broomall, PA: Mason Crest Publishers, 2007.

Masar, Brenden. *Usher*. Detroit, MI: Lucent Books, 2007.

Web Sites:

Usher
www.usherworld.com

Usher
www.mtv.com/music/artist/usher/artist.jhtml

Glossary

charts: lists of songs or albums that have sold well

confession: a telling of the bad things one has done

Grammy: an honor given to someone for their music

musical: a play that uses singing, music, and dancing to tell a story

R&B: a short way to say rhythm and blues. This kind of music has a strong beat and is sometimes sad.

Index